動字文英感動

1000

ACTION
WORDS

Illustrated by
May Kong

Edited by Valerie Barth

THE COMMERCIAL PRESS (HONG KONG) LTD.

earlybird books
An imprint of Federal Publications

A Note to Parents

Action words are verbs — those important words in the English Language without which no sentence is complete. Verbs form an important part of a child's vocabulary. They help children to talk about the things that people do and the things that happen around them.

This book is designed to introduce to children 1000 of the more common verbs in the English Language. We have included both single-word verbs, e.g. **call**, as well as phrasal verbs, e.g. **call off**.

The book has been prepared with three principal aims in mind:
- to enlarge the child's vocabulary of verbs;
- to show the subtle differences between verbs that are similar in meaning, e.g. **see**, **look**, **glare**, **stare**;
- to introduce to the child the meanings of useful phrasal verbs such as **get away**, **get off**, **get on** and **get up**.

Please note, however, that the action words have not been listed in strict alphabetical order. While the words have been grouped according to their initial letters, within each group they have been arranged in a context which is more logical or more visually appealing than a strict alphabetical listing would allow.

Each entry is accompanied by a sentence which demonstrates the way in which the action word is typically used in the context of everyday speech. The lively and amusing illustrations will certainly appeal to children and make the learning of new action words an enjoyable experience.

© **1988 The Commercial Press (Hong Kong) Ltd.**
This edition first published 1988 jointly by
The Commercial Press (Hong Kong) Ltd.
4/F., Kiu Ying Bldg., 2D Finnie Street, Quarry Bay, Hong Kong
and Federal Publications (S) Pte Ltd., 1 New Industrial Road, Singapore 1953

Originally entitled *TIMES 1000 Action Words*

Reprinted 1990
ISBN 962 07 0098 8
Printed by Times Offset Pte Ltd

Aa

accept accepting, accepted
Kathy **accepts** a gift from her father.

answer
answering, answered
Helen is **answering** the telephone.

add adding, added
Mother is **adding** some milk to her coffee.

attend attending, attended
We are **attending** Jane's birthday party.

add up
Teacher asked me to **add up** these numbers.

act acting, acted
Jimmy **acted** as a wolf in the school play.

Little Red Riding Hood

awake awaking, awoke
The alarm clock **awoke** me from sleep.

admire admiring, admired
Jane's friends **admire** her beautiful new doll.

arrive arriving, arrived

We **arrived** at the station too late.
The train had left without us.

Will you help me with my bags?

Yes

agree
agreeing, agreed

Peter **agreed** to help me with my bags.

aim aiming, aimed

Andy **aims** carefully at the apple.

arrange arranging, arranged

Father is **arranging** the bags on the shelf.

Gate 2

advise advising, advised

The policeman **advised** us to cross the road carefully.

allow allowing, allowed

Dogs are not **allowed** in this station.

2

appear appearing, appeared
A bright star **appeared** suddenly in the sky.

attack attacking, attacked
The fierce dog **attacked** the burglar.

announce announcing, announced
The station master **announces** the arrival of the train.

amuse amusing, amused
The clown **amused** us with his tricks.

annoy annoying, annoyed
Kathy is **annoyed** at her brother for spilling coffee over her favourite dress.

ache aching, ached
Willy's stomach **aches** because he ate too much.

ask asking, asked
I **asked** mother for another slice of cake.

3

Bb

bleed bleeding, bled
Jimmy's arm is **bleeding**.

bandage bandaging, bandaged
The nurse is **bandaging** Jimmy's arm.

bake baking, baked
Mother is **baking** a cake for Kathy's birthday.

belong belonging, belonged
This book **belongs** to me.
It is mine.

barbecue
barbecuing, barbecued
Father is **barbecuing** in the backyard.

bark barking, barked
The dogs are **barking** loudly at the cat.

bath bathing, bathed
Mother **baths** the baby in warm water.

beat beating, beat
Mandy is **beating** an egg.

Jimmy is **beating** the drum.

Helen **beats** Willy in the race.

4

break
breaking, broke
Willy **broke** the stick into two pieces.

break down
Father's car **broke down** on his way to work.

blush   **blushing, blushed**
Linda **blushed** when Jimmy gave her a kiss.

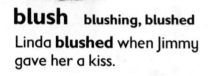

bend   **bending, bent**
Willy is **bending** a stick.

Benny **bends** down to pick a coin.

block   **blocking, blocked**
The fallen tree is **blocking** the road.

box   **boxing, boxed**
That big boy **boxed** Andy on the chin.

bounce   **bouncing, bounced**
Andy is **bouncing** a ball.

bow   **bowing, bowed**
The magician is **bowing** to the audience.

button
buttoning, buttoned
Helen is **buttoning** up her jacket.

5

beg begging, begged
The clever dog **begs** for a bone.

bring bringing, brought
Mother is **bringing** us some food.

boil boiling, boiled
The water is **boiling**.
Mother will switch the kettle off.

borrow borrowing, borrowed
Helen is **borrowing** books from the library.

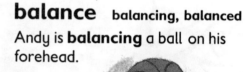

balance balancing, balanced
Andy is **balancing** a ball on his forehead.

Uncle Roy is **blowing** his nose.
He has a cold.

blow blowing, blew
The wind is **blowing** through the trees.

blow up
Andy is **blowing up** a balloon.

blow out
Jane **blows out** the candles on her birthday cake.

bite biting, bit
The dog is **biting** a bone.

6

bury
burying, buried
The dog is **burying** a bone.

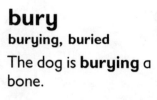

burn   burning, burnt
Father is **burning** some leaves.

brush   brushing, brushed
Jimmy is **brushing** his teeth.
Kathy is **brushing** her hair.

breathe   breathing, breathed
We **breathe** through our noses.

burst   bursting, burst
The balloon **burst** with a loud bang.

bump   bumping, bumped
Willy **bumped** into a street lamp.

build   building, built
Peter is **building** a spaceship.

buy   buying, bought
Mandy is **buying** some flowers.

bully   bullying, bullied
That big boy is **bullying** the little children.

7

Cc

camp   camping, camped
The scouts **camped** at the beach.

call   calling, called
Call the firemen to put out the fire.

help!

call for
Willy **called for** help when he got into trouble while swimming.

call off
The teacher had to **call off** the picnic because it was raining.

catch   catching, caught
Jimmy held out both hands to **catch** the ball.

care   caring, cared
Simon **cares** for his pet rabbit. He feeds it and cleans its cage every day.

change   changing, changed
Willy **changed** out of his wet clothes into dry ones.

catch up
The snail cannot **catch up** with the rabbit.
He is too slow.

cause   causing, caused
Willy's sneeze **caused** the glass of water to fall over.

carry   carrying, carried
Mother is **carrying** the baby.

carry on
Grandmother let me **carry on** watching television although it was past my bedtime.

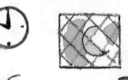

celebrate
celebrating, celebrated
Jane is **celebrating** her birthday by having a party.

chat   chatting, chatted
Kathy is **chatting** with her friends.

cheat   cheating, cheated
Jimmy **cheated** at cards.

choose   choosing, chose
It is hard to **choose** which sweets to buy when they all look so nice.

chip   chipping, chipped
Andy dropped a plate and **chipped** it.

7 + 8 = ?
(a) 5   (b) 10   (c) 15

chase   chasing, chased
The dog **chased** the cat up a tree.

carve   carving, carved
Peter is **carving** a piece of wood into a boat.

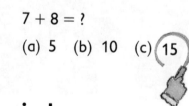

circle   circling, circled
Helen is **circling** the right answer to the sum.

check   checking, checked
Linda is counting her school books to **check** if she has them all.

check in
We **checked in** to the hotel at the start of our holiday.

check out
We were sad to **check out** of the hotel at the end of our holiday.

cling   clinging, clung
The baby koala **clings** tightly to its mother.

check up
We are going to see a movie tonight. Simon is **checking up** on the times of the shows.

chop
chopping, chopped
Uncle Roy **chopped** down the tree.

charge
charging, charged
The rhinoceros **charged** at the fence.

cheer   cheering, cheered
The girls are **cheering** their team at the race.

cheer up
The cartoon show **cheered up** the children and made them laugh.

clap   clapping, clapped
When the show ended, the children **clapped** their hands.

clean up
Mother told Jimmy to **clean up** his room.

clean cleaning, cleaned
Father **cleans** the car on Sundays.

chew chewing, chewed
The dog is **chewing** a bone.

clear clearing, cleared
I am **clearing** the desk so that I have room to do my homework.

clear away
Kathy helps father **clear away** the dishes after dinner.

clear up
The children are **clearing up** the mess after the funfair.

clear off
The thief **cleared off** when he saw a policeman coming.

clear out
Dad is **clearing out** the garage.

climb climbing, climbed
The baby **climbed** up a chair.

cluck clucking, clucked
A hen **clucks** loudly after it has laid an egg.

complain
complaining, complained

Kathy **complained** to mother that Andy had torn her book.

clip clipping, clipped

Mandy is **clipping** the papers together so that they will not get lost.

collect
collecting, collected

Peter **collects** stamps from around the world.

colour colouring, coloured

Andy is **colouring** a picture of a lion.

comb combing, combed

Jane is **combing** her long hair.

coach coaching, coached

Mr Thomson **coaches** the soccer team.
He shows them how to kick the ball.

congratulate
congratulating, congratulated

Everyone **congratulated** the winner.

close closing, closed
Mother is **closing** the door.

coil coiling, coiled

Father **coiled** the garden hose after he had watered the plants.

collapse collapsing, collapsed
The tent **collapsed** in the strong wind.

confuse confusing, confused

The signs **confused** the driver.

collide colliding, collided

The car **collided** with a van.

compare

comparing, compared

Benny is tall **compared** with Helen.

come coming, came

Come with me.
I'll show you the way.

come off

A button **came off** Kathy's coat.

come apart

The shirt was too small and **came apart** at the seam when Willy put it on.

come out

The moon and star **come out** at night.

come across

Andy **came across** a gold chain while looking for his lost marble.

come back

Boomerangs always **come back** when thrown.

come on

The magician **came on** the stage wearing a long black cape.

13

connect

connecting, connected

Uncle Roy **connected** the aerial to the television.

consider

considering, considered

Mother and father are **considering** what to get for Kathy for her birthday.

consist

consisting, consisted

This gift set **consists** of two storybooks and two tapes.

construct

constructing, constructed

Peter **constructed** a spaceship from clothes pegs.

continue

continuing, continued

"Mother, don't stop now. Please **continue** reading the story," the children asked.

control

controlling, controlled

Andy **controls** the robot by remote control.

cool   cooling, cooled

Mandy is **cooling** her feet in the stream.

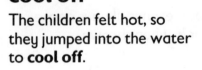

cool off

The children felt hot, so they jumped into the water to **cool off**.

cool down

The porridge was hot, so the three bears left it to **cool down**.

contain
containing, contained

This bottle **contains** ink.

cover
covering, covered

Kathy **covered** her face with her hands.

cover up

Andy **covered up** the ink stain so his mother would not see it.

copy
copying, copied

Linda **copied** the sums from the blackboard.

contribute
contributing contributed

The children **contributed** some money to buy a present for their mother.

cook
cooking, cooked

Mother **cooked** a delicious roast chicken.

cost
costing, cost

This hamburger **costs** $1.30.

count
counting, counted

The rich man is **counting** his money.

cough
coughing, coughed

Willy **coughed** because he had a sore throat.

crack
cracking, cracked

The vase **cracked** when it was dropped.

crash crashing, crashed
The car **crashed** into the wall.

create creating, created
The magician **created** a monster with his spells.

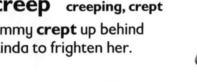

crawl crawling, crawled
The baby is **crawling** across the room.

crouch
crouching, crouched
Kathy **crouched** behind a chair to hide from Willy.

creep creeping, crept
Jimmy **crept** up behind Linda to frighten her.

cross crossing, crossed
We looked left and right before **crossing** the street.

croak croaking, croaked
The frogs are **croaking** a song.

cry crying, cried
Jane **cried** when she fell down and hurt her knee.

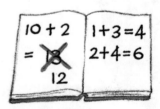

cross out
Peter **crossed out** a mistake in his book.

16

crumple

crumpling, crumpled

Andy **crumpled** up the drawing.

cuddle cuddling, cuddled

The baby is **cuddling** a teddy bear.

crumble crumbling, crumbled

Mother is **crumbling** the biscuit into a bowl.

crow crowing, crowed

The rooster **crows** loudly in the early morning.

cycle cycling, cycled

Bobby **cycles** home from school.

crush crushing, crushed

The soccer ball was **crushed** by the steam roller.

curl curling, curled

The cat **curled** up on the cushion.

curtsy curtsying, curtsied

Cinderella **curtsied** to the queen.

crowd crowding, crowded

The children are **crowding** around the friendly chimpanzee.

cut cutting, cut
Aunt Molly is **cutting** the cake into slices.

cut down
Father **cut down** a tree in the garden.

cut off
Bobby is **cutting off** the sleeves from his T-shirt.

cut out
Linda is **cutting out** pictures from a magazine.

cut up
Kathy **cuts up** the vegetables to make a salad.

Dd

damage damaging, damaged
The ship was **damaged** when it hit the rocks.

dance dancing, danced
The children are **dancing** happily round the Christmas tree.

dare daring, dared
Andy didn't **dare** touch the snake.

darn darning, darned
Mother is **darning** a hole in Jimmy's sock.

dash dashing, dashed
The dog **dashed** across the street.

describe
describing, described

Jimmy is **describing** to the policeman the dog that he has lost.

demand
demanding, demanded

The spoilt child **demanded** the biggest ice-cream.

decorate
decorating, decorated

Mandy is **decorating** the hall.

delight
delighting, delighted

Jane was **delighted** with her new puppy.

deliver
delivering, delivered

The postman **delivered** a parcel to Linda's house.

decide deciding, decided
Helen could not **decide** whether to wear shorts or a dress.

deal dealing, dealt
You **deal** all the cards to play Snap.

deserve deserving, deserved
Bobby practised hard for the swimming contest and **deserved** first prize.

defend   defending, defended
The soldiers are **defending** their country from attack.

die   dying, died
The bear **died** after the hunter shot it.

develop
developing, developed
The bodybuilder **developed** huge muscles.

die down
We let the fire **die down** after the barbecue.

die away
The music **died away** at the end of the song.

destroy   destroying, destroyed
The big boy **destroyed** Andy's sandcastle.

dig   digging, dug
Uncle Roy is **digging** a hole to plant the tree.

dial   dialing, dialed
Helen **dialed** 999 to call the police.

design   designing, designed
Aunt Molly is **designing** a party dress for Kathy.

demonstrate
demonstrating, demonstrated
The fireman **demonstrated** how to put out the fire.

20

disguise

disguising, disguised

The thief **disguised** himself as an old lady.

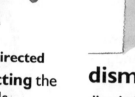

direct

directing, directed

The policeman is **directing** the traffic at the crossroads.

dismiss

dismissing, dismissed

At the end of the day the children are **dismissed** from class.

disappear

disappearing, disappeared

The wizard **disappeared** in a puff of smoke.

discover

discovering, discovered

The scientist **discovered** a new plant in the forest.

dip

dipping, dipped

The cat **dipped** its paw into the fish tank to try to catch a fish.

display

displaying, displayed

The new books are **displayed** in the shop window.

disturb

disturbing, disturbed

Do not **disturb** Dad. He is sleeping.

discuss

discussing, discussed

Willy, Linda and Jimmy **discussed** where they wanted to go for a picnic.

do doing, did

Jimmy must **do** his homework. He cannot play with Andy now.

dream

dreaming, dreamed or **dreamt**

Helen **dreams** of being a pilot.

dock docking, docked

The ship **docked** at the wharf to unload its cargo.

dislike disliking, disliked

Andy **dislikes** vegetables.

do away

Jack **did away** with the giant.

do up

Bobby **did up** an old bike. Now it looks like new.

dress dressing, dressed

Linda **dressed** as a witch for Halloween.

donate donating, donated

Mandy **donated** her savings to the old folk's home.

divide dividing, divided

Jimmy is **dividing** the sweets into two equal piles.

dive diving, dived

Bobby is **diving** into the pool.

drag dragging, dragged
The men are **dragging** the boat up onto the beach.

drift drifting, drifted
There was no wind and the boat **drifted** on the sea.

drown
drowning, drowned
The lifeguard rescued Willy who was **drowning**.

draw drawing, drew
Andy is **drawing** a rabbit.

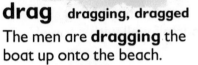

drill drilling, drilled
Uncle Roy is **drilling** a hole in the wall.

doze dozing, dozed
Dogs love to **doze** in the sun.

drive driving, drove
Father **drives** the car to work each morning.

drip dripping, dripped
Water is **dripping** from the ceiling onto the floor.

doodle doodling, doodled
Helen is **doodling** on a piece of paper.

drain draining, drained
Kathy let the dishes **drain** after she washed them.

drink drinking, drank

Willy **drank** a glass of milk with breakfast.

drink up

The elephant **drank up** all the water in the bucket.

dry drying, dried

After a bath, you **dry** yourself well with a towel.

dust dusting, dusted

Mother is **dusting** the furniture.

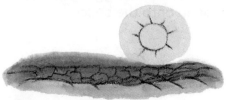

dry out

The puddle **dried out** in the hot sun

duck ducking, ducked

The giant **ducked** his head to get through the door.

drop off

Mother **dropped** Kathy **off** at school.

dump

dumping, dumped

The truck **dumped** the rubbish in a heap.

drop in

Andy **dropped in** to see his grandmother.

drop dropping, dropped

Linda **dropped** an egg on the floor.

Ee

edge   edging, edged
The clown **edged** his way carefully along the narrow plank.

eat   eating, ate
Elephants **eat** a lot.

eat up
The mouse **ate up** all the cheese.

elect   electing, elected
The team **elected** the captain from among themselves.

emerge   emerging, emerged
Suddenly a shark **emerged** from the water.

embrace
embracing, embraced
Father **embraced** mother lovingly.

embarrass

embarrassing, embarrassed

Andy **embarrassed** his father by being rude in front of Aunt Molly.

earn   earning earned
Bobby **earns** pocket money by washing cars.

entertain
entertaining, entertained
The clown **entertained** us with his funny tricks.

escape
escaping, escaped
The monkey **escaped** from the cage.

engrave
engraving, engraved
Andy is **engraving** his name in the tree trunk.

enjoy
enjoying, enjoyed
Mandy **enjoys** watching television.

enter
entering, entered
The burglar is **entering** the house by the window.

employ
employing, employed
Sam is **employed** to clean windows.

empty
emptying, emptied
The baby **emptied** the box of blocks onto the floor.

$$1 + 1 = 2$$

equal
equalling, equalled
One and one **equals** two.

end
ending, ended
The road **ends** at the cliff edge.

erase
erasing, erased
It is easy to **erase** mistakes with a rubber.

examine examining, examined
The doctor is **examining** the sick boy.

explain
explaining, explained
The teacher **explained** to the children how to jump over the hurdles.

excuse excusing, excused
Jane is **excused** from sports because she has hurt her ankle.

excite
exciting, excited
Mandy was **excited** when she saw the gold cup.

exercise
exercising, exercised
Bobby **exercises** everyday to keep fit.

expect expecting, expected
I **expect** it will rain today. There are a lot of dark clouds in the sky.

expand
expanding, expanded
A balloon **expands** when you blow it up.

explore
exploring, explored
Kathy is **exploring** the rock pools looking for crabs.

exchange exchanging, exchanged
Willy is **exchanging** shorts with Peter.

27

Ff

face up
It is hard to **face up** to your teacher when you have not done your homework.

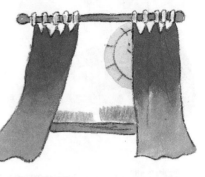

fade fading, faded
The curtains have **faded**.

face facing, faced
Linda **faced** the clock to see what time it was.

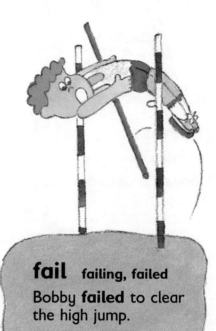

fall falling, fell
Willy tripped over a stone and **fell** on his hands and knees.

fall off
Andy **fell off** his chair in fright.

faint fainting, fainted
Mandy saw a ghost and **fainted**.

fake faking, faked
Andy **faked** a stomachache because he did not want to go to school.

fan fanning, fanned
Aunt Molly **fanned** herself to keep cool.

fail failing, failed
Bobby **failed** to clear the high jump.

28

fast fasting, fasted
The holy man is **fasting**.
He is not eating any food.

farm farming, farmed
Uncle Roy **farms** a small piece
of land behind the house.

feed feeding, fed
Simon **feeds** his pet rabbit
carrots and lettuce.

feel feeling, felt
Rabbits **feel** soft and
cuddly.

fear fearing, feared
Kathy **fears** snakes.

fetch fetching, fetched
The dog **fetches** the stick for
Jimmy.

feel like
On a hot day we **feel like**
a cold drink.

fasten fastening, fastened
Willy is **fastening** his seat
belt.

find finding, found
Mandy **found** a coin on the
footpath.

find out
Jimmy looked in the phone
book to **find out** Peter's
phone number.

fit fitting, fitted
Cinderella's foot **fitted** the shoe perfectly.

fit in
Only five people could **fit in** the car.

finish finishing, finished
The rabbit **finished** first in the race.

finish with
Helen had **finished with** the book, so she returned it to the library.

fill filling, filled
Andy is **filling** the pool with water.

fill up
Jane **filled up** the bucket with sand.

fence fencing, fenced
Uncle Roy is **fencing** the tree with wire.

fight fighting, fought
Bobby and Jimmy are **fighting**.

film filming, filmed
They are **filming** a fight.

30

flap flapping, flapped
The washing is **flapping** in the wind.

flag flagging, flagged
The people **flag** the buildings to celebrate the king's birthday.

flag down
We **flag down** a taxi.

flash flashing, flashed
The light from the lighthouse **flashed** across the sea.

flow flowing, flowed
The river **flows** down to the sea.

float floating, floated
Kathy can **float** on her back.

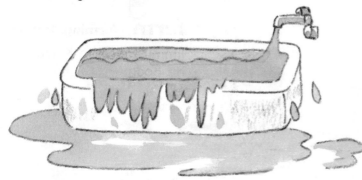

flood flooding, flooded
Andy left the tap on and **flooded** the floor.

flush flushing, flushed
Jane is **flushing** the toilet.

31

fizz fizzing, fizzed
This drink **fizzes** for a while when I pour it out.

flatten flattening, flattened
Willy **flattened** the plasticine.

fold folding, folded
Andy **folded** a piece of paper to make a dart.

flip flipping, flipped
I can **flip** a coin in the air.

fix fixing, fixed
Helen is **fixing** lunch.

freeze freezing, froze
When water **freezes** it becomes ice.

fling flinging, flung
The lazy boy **flung** his clothes on the floor.

foam foaming, foamed
The beer **foams** over the glass.

form forming, formed
Jimmy **forms** a K with his body.

forget forgetting, forgot
Poor Willy cannot write. He has **forgotten** to bring his pencil.

frown frowning, frowned
Bobby **frowns** when he is worried.

32

fire firing, fired
The hunter is **firing** at the birds.

fly flying, flew
Birds **fly** in the sky.

fish fishing, fished
Jimmy likes to **fish** with his father.

flick flicking, flicked
The cow is **flicking** the flies with its tail.

fluff fluffing, fluffed
The hen is **fluffing** out its feathers.

flit flitting, flitted
The butterfly **flits** from flower to flower.

flee fleeing, fled
The animals are **fleeing** from the burning forest.

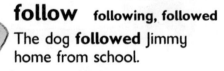

follow following, followed
The dog **followed** Jimmy home from school.

free freeing, freed
Linda is **freeing** the bird from its cage.

33

Gg

frighten
frightening, frightened
Little Miss Muffet was **frightened** by the spider.

gallop
galloping, galloped
Jimmy was afraid when his horse **galloped** down the hill.

gamble
gambling gambled
These men are **gambling**.

fry
frying, fried
Mother is **frying** an egg for Andy.

garden
gardening, gardened
Father is **gardening**. He is planting roses.

gather
gathering, gathered
Grandfather **gathered** fruit from the trees.

furnish
furnishing, furnished
Aunt Molly **furnished** her room with a bed, dressing table and chair.

gasp
gasping, gasped
The water was so cold, Bobby **gasped** with shock.

gaze
gazing, gazed
Kathy is **gazing** at the stars.

34

give giving, gave
Mother **gave** Andy a bag.

give away
Jimmy didn't want his pencils so he **gave** them **away**.

give up
The robber **gave** himself **up** to the police.

give back
The teacher is **giving back** the exercise books.

give out
The headmaster is **giving out** prizes to the best pupils.

give off
A fire **gives off** smoke.

glue glueing, glued
Kathy **glued** a picture in the book.

glare glaring, glared
The two boys have stopped fighting, but they are still **glaring**.

glow glowing, glowed
The cat's eyes **glow** in the dark.

35

get getting, got

Jimmy **got** a pail of water from the river.

get down

Simon climbed a tree and couldn't **get down**.

get away

Get away from the fire! You might get hurt.

get on

Linda **got on** the horse without any help.

get at

Andy cannot **get at** the bird.

get back

The runners were tired when they **got back** from the cross-country run.

get across

Jimmy **got across** the river on a bridge.

get over

Peter couldn't **get over** the wall.

get off

Bobby **got off** the bus at the swimming pool.

get around

Pilots **get around** a lot.
They visit many countries.

get up

Andy **gets up** at 7 o'clock.

get in

Ali Baba **got in** a jar to hide from the thieves.

get dressed

It is late.
You must **get dressed** at once.

giggle   giggling, giggled

The playful puppy made
Kathy **giggle**.

get into

Father **got into** the car
and drove off.

get along

Helen is a sweet girl who **gets along**
with all her classmates.

go going, went

Andy **goes** for a drive in his toy car.

glide gliding, glided

A paper aeroplane **glides** through the air.

go back

Linda forgot her umbrella. She **went back** home for it.

go out

Mr and Mrs Brown are **going out** to a party.

go away

"**Go away!**" said Jane. "I want to be alone."

go on

Mandy **went on** the roller coaster.

go without

Andy was naughty and had to **go without** dinner.

grill grilling, grilled

Father is **grilling** some sausages.

grip gripping, gripped

Kathy **gripped** her mother's arm when they were on the ferris wheel.

grin grinning, grinned

Willy is **grinning** because his mother has given him a toy.

grind grinding, ground

The cook is **grinding** nuts.

38

grab grabbing, grabbed
The thief **grabbed** Aunt Molly's handbag.

growl growling, growled
The guard dog **growled** at the stranger.

grunt grunting, grunted
When pigs are hungry they **grunt**.

group grouping, grouped
Simon **grouped** the toy animals into pets and wild animals.

grow growing, grew
Potatoes **grow** under the ground.

greet greeting, greeted
We **greeted** Grandmother with a bunch of flowers.

guard guarding, guarded
The soldiers **guard** the jewels from thieves.

guide guiding, guided
The boy scout **guided** the blind man across the street.

gush gushing, gushed
Look! The water is **gushing** out of the broken pipe.

guess guessing, guessed
Close your eyes and **guess** what your present is.

gum gumming, gummed
Linda **gummed** the two cards together to make a thicker card.

Hh

hack hacking, hacked
The fireman **hacked** the door with an axe.

halt halting, halted
"**Halt!**" said the fireman. "You cannot enter."

halve halving, halved
Mandy **halved** the orange before squeezing out the juice.

handle handling, handled
Linda **handled** the glasses with great care.

hail hailing, hailed
Aunt Molly **hailed** a taxi to take her home.

handcuff handcuffing, handcuffed
The policeman **handcuffed** the thief.

hammer
hammering, hammered

Jimmy **hammered** a nail into the wood.

hand handing, handed
The postman **handed** the letter to Kathy.

hand out
Mother is **handing out** sweets to the children.

hang hanging, hung

Andy **hung** his shirt up in the cupboard.

has has, having

Jimmy **has** a blue cap.

has to

We **have to** drink water everyday.

has got

Willy **has got** chicken pox.

harvest harvesting, harvested

The farmer is **harvesting** the crop.

hatch hatching, hatched

The chicks **hatched** out of the eggs.

hate hating, hated

Willy **hates** to wake up early on cold mornings.

heal healing, healed

The cut on my arm has **healed**. I can take off the plaster.

harm harming, harmed

Is the big bad wolf going to **harm** Red Riding Hood?

haul hauling, hauled

The fishermen **hauled** their net onto the boat.

heat
heating, heated
The fire **heats** the soup to boiling point.

hear   hearing, heard
Mother **heard** the baby cry.

hiccup
hiccupping, hiccupped
Poor Andy is **hiccupping**. How can he stop it?

hide   hiding, hid
The cat is **hiding** under a chair.

heap
heaping, heaped
Kathy **heaped** her clothes on the floor.

help   helping, helped
Kathy **helps** her mother make the bed.

head   heading, headed
Jimmy **headed** the ball into the goal.

The last time I saw Bobby, he was **heading** for home.

hiss   hissing, hissed
The snake **hissed** when Andy stepped on it.

hit   hitting, hit
Willy **hit** the ball with the baseball bat.

42

hike hiking, hiked
We **hiked** round the lake the whole day.

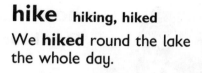

hire hiring, hired
The tourist **hired** a car for $50 a week.

hold out
Willy **held out** his hand. He wanted to shake Mandy's hand.

hold holding, held
Andy is **holding** a baby orangutan's hand.

hold on
Kathy **held on** tightly as her father carried her on his back.

hoist hoisting, hoisted
Look! Bobby is **hoisting** the school flag.

hold up
Two masked men **held up** the cashier and took all the money.

hope hoping, hoped
Linda **hoped** the postman would bring a letter.

43

hoot hooting, hooted
Owls **hoot** at night.

hook hooking, hooked
Jimmy has **hooked** a big fish.

honk honking, honked
Geese **honk** at strangers.

hum humming, hummed
Willy is **humming** as he walks
to the park.

hop hopping, hopped
The children are **hopping**
around the playground.

hurl hurling, hurled
Jimmy **hurled** the ball
as far as he could.

hurt hurting, hurt
Simon **hurt** his toe on a rock.

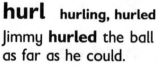

huff huffing, huffed
The children **huffed** and
puffed after the run.

huddle huddling, huddled
The chicks are **huddling**
together to keep warm.

hose hosing, hosed
Father is **hosing** the car down.

howl howling, howled
The baby **howled** when it fell out of its cot.

hurry hurrying, hurried
Jimmy got up late and **hurried** to get dressed.

hurry up
Hurry up if you want to get to school on time!

hunt hunting, hunted
Grandmother is **hunting** for her glasses.

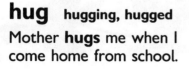

hug hugging, hugged
Mother **hugs** me when I come home from school.

hush hushing, hushed
Hush! Don't wake the baby.

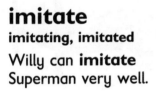

Ii

imitate
imitating, imitated

Willy can **imitate** Superman very well.

inspect inspecting, inspected
Bobby dropped his kite.
He **inspected** it to make sure that it was all right.

injure
injuring, injured

Simon fell down and **injured** his arm.

inform informing, informed
The teacher **informed** the children where to go to fly their kites.

itch itching, itched
Peter's arm **itches** because a mosquito bit him there.

invent inventing, invented
The scientist **invented** a machine to walk a dog.

imagine
imagining, imagined

Kathy **imagined** she was a movie star.

interrupt
interrupting, interrupted

Andy **interrupted** his teacher who was talking.

instruct   instructing, instructed
The teacher is **instructing** the children how to fly a kite.

introduce   introducing, introduced
Mandy **introduced** Terry to Jimmy.

install   installing, installed
The workers are **installing** a new pole.

interview
interviewing, interviewed

The reporter **interviewed** Bobby.
He asked him about the party.

increase
increasing, increased

If you blow more air into the balloon, its size will **increase**.

I'm pleased to have been invited to this party.

invite
inviting, invited

Bobby was **invited** to a fancy-dress party.

iron   ironing, ironed
Father is **ironing** his shirt.

Jj

judge
judging, judged
Kathy's dog was **judged** the best dog in the show.

join
joining, joined
Willy can **join** two pieces of string with a knot.

jingle
jingling, jingled
There are bells on the dog's collar. They **jingle** when it moves.

jump to
The dogs **jumped to** attention when the judge arrived.

jump
jumping, jumped
The cat **jumped** over the sleeping dog and ran off as quickly as it could.

jump at
The dog **jumped at** the man passing by.

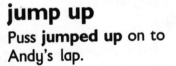

jump up
Puss **jumped up** on to Andy's lap.

jack up
Father **jacked up** the car to change the tyre.

jerk jerking, jerked
The car **jerked** a few times and then stopped suddenly.

joke joking, joked
The children are **joking** with one another.
They are telling funny stories.

jumble
jumbling, jumbled

The naughty girl **jumbled** her clothes up.

juggle juggling, juggled
The clown is **juggling** six balls.

jam jamming, jammed
Andy **jammed** the clothes in the suitcase.

jog jogging, jogged
Bobby **jogged** around the track.

jot jotting, jotted
Peter **jotted** down my phone number on a piece of paper.

Kk

kick kicking, kicked
Terry **kicked** the ball over the fence.

keep keeping, kept
Helen **keeps** her pet snake in a basket.

keep up
Bobby can run faster than Willy. Willy can't **keep up** with him.

keep away
Keep away from the dog. It bites!

keep off
Keep off the grass. There are prickles.

knock knocking, knocked

The postman is **knocking** on the door. He has a parcel to deliver.

kill killing, killed
The prince became a hero when he **killed** a dragon.

50

kneel kneeling, knelt
Jimmy **kneels** down to pray.

kiss kissing, kissed
Mother **kissed** Kathy on her cheek.

knit knitting, knitted
Grandmother is **knitting** a jumper.

knot knotting, knotted
Mandy is **knotting** a scarf round her neck.

4 + 4 = 8

know knowing, knew
Peter **knows** the answer to the sum.

Ll

ladle ladling, ladled
The old woman is **ladling** out soup to the children.

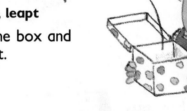

leap leaping, leapt
Helen opened the box and a frog **leapt** out.

laugh laughing, laughed
Andy is **laughing** because Jane is tickling him.

ha ha ha ha

laugh at
The children are **laughing at** the clown's tricks.

51

lead up to
The winding path **leads up to** the haunted house.

lead   leading, led
Andy is **leading** his dog up the winding path.

last   lasting, lasted
I wonder how long the rain will **last**.

lay   laying, laid
Kathy is **laying** the table for dinner.

Our hen **lays** two eggs every day.

leak   leaking, leaked
The roof is **leaking**.

lean
leaning, leaned or leant
The ladder **leans** against the wall.

leave out
The boys were playing marbles and Linda was **left out**.

leave   leaving, left
Willy **left** his school bag at the bus stop.

land   landing, landed
Bobby's ball **landed** in Aunt Molly's soup.

52

learn learning, learned or learnt
Jane is **learning** how to play the piano.

lend lending, lent
Mandy **lent** Linda her music book.

like liking, liked
Jimmy **likes** the trumpet.
Kathy **likes** the flute.

listen listening, listened
Andy is **listening** to the radio.

let letting, let
The teacher **let** Andy play the guitar.

let down
Rapunzel **let down** her long hair.

let go
Bobby **let go** of the balloon and it floated away.

let in
Open the door and **let** Simon **in**.

let out
Willy **let out** a cry of pain when he hit his finger.

53

I didn't break it.

lie lying, lied
Andy is **lying**.

The cat is **lying** in the washing basket.

lie down
Grandmother is tired.
She is **lying down** on the sofa.

light lighting, lighted
Grandfather is very careful when he **lights** the candle.

link linking, linked
The new road **links** the two towns.

lose losing, lost
Jimmy dropped $10 and **lost** it.

list listing, listed
Aunt Molly is **listing** the things she needs to buy.

limp limping, limped
The dog has a sore paw and is **limping**.

lift lifting, lifted
Willy **lifted** Jimmy up.

54

lick   licking, licked
Andy is **licking** a lollipop.

litter   littering, littered
Andy has **littered** the floor with sweet wrappers.

long   longing, longed
Andy is **longing** for chocolate. It's his favourite food.

line   lining, lined
Kathy is **lining** the shelf with paper.

line up
Mandy **lined up** the chairs for the concert.

loll   lolling, lolled
Willy is **lolling** on the sofa, doing nothing.

live   living, lived
There was an old woman who **lived** in a shoe.

live on
Monkeys **live on** fruit and nuts.

look looking, looked
Look at the aeroplane flying upside down.

look out
Look out! A branch is falling down.

look after
Mother **looks after** the baby all day.

look for
The children are **looking for** the lost ball.

look up
Helen doesn't know how to spell a word.
She is **looking** it **up** in the dictionary.

lock up
Aunt Molly **locks up** her jewels in a safe.

lock locking, locked
Every night father **locks** the door.

load loading, loaded
The men are **loading** the van with sacks of flour.

loop looping, looped
The cowboy **loops** the rope round the bull.

Mm

mail mailing, mailed
Kathy has written a letter to her friend.
She is **mailing** it.

mount
mounting, mounted
Bobby is **mounting** his bicycle.

love loving, loved
I **love** my grandmother.

mark marking, marked
The teacher is **marking** the exercise books.

mow mowing, mowed
Father is **mowing** the lawn.

lunch lunching, lunched
Andy is **lunching** with his aunt.

mash mashing, mashed

Jimmy is **mashing** the potatoes.

measure

measuring, measured

Andy is **measuring** the flour with a cup.

melt melting, melted

Ice **melts** when you take it out of the freezer.

make of

This jar is **made of** glass.

make making, made

Willy is **making** a sandwich for himself.

make off

The thief **made off** with a big cake.

make from

This jam is **made from** strawberries.

make out

The stranger wore a mask and Helen couldn't **make out** who he was.

make for

Jimmy **made for** the door when Linda ran after him with a rolling pin.

mince   mincing, minced
Simon is **mincing** the meat
to make pies.

mix   mixing, mixed
Willy **mixed** flour and
water to make a dough.

mend   mending, mended
Bobby is **mending** the
broken toaster.

mistake   mistaking, mistook
Andy **mistook** pepper for salt.

mess up
The wind **messed up** Kathy's
hair.

mew   mewing, mewed
The cat is **mewing**.
It wants food.

mop   mopping, mopped
Peter is **mopping** the floor
to clean off his dirty
footprints.

mime   miming, mimed
Andy is **miming** that he wants a drink.

match   matching, matched
Jimmy's socks do not **match**.

model
modelling, modelled
Kathy is **modelling**
a party dress.

marry   marrying, married
Aunt Jane **married** a soldier.

miss   missing, missed
The paper aeroplane just
missed Linda's head.

miss out
When the teacher was giving the children
crayons, he **missed out** Willy.

mask   masking, masked
The children **mask** their
faces for the party.

meet   meeting, met
Bobby **met** Mandy
outside the post office.

march   marching, marched
The band **marched** down
the street playing music.

moo
mooing, mooed
Cows **moo.**

milk milking, milked
The farmer is **milking** the cow.

mine mining, mined
The miners are **mining** coal from under the ground.

move moving, moved
Jimmy picked up his books and **moved** them to another desk.

move in
Mr and Mrs Sharp are **moving in** next door.

move out
Bobby is **moving out** of the haunted house.

Nn

nap napping, napped
Willy is **napping** in the garden.

nail nailing, nailed
The workman is **nailing** a sign on the fence.

nod nodding, nodded
Uncle Roy is **nodding** his head to show that he wants the coffee.

Would you like some coffee?

nudge nudging, nudged
Uncle Roy is **nudging** a workman who has fallen asleep.

nip nipping, nipped
The dog is **nipping** the man on the leg.

need needing, needed
This workman **needs** a new pair of shoes.

neigh neighing, neighed
Horses **neigh**.

notice noticing, noticed
Mr Trump **noticed** a man sneaking out through the back gate.

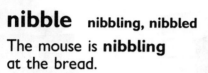

nibble nibbling, nibbled
The mouse is **nibbling** at the bread.

name naming, named
The baby was **named** Melissa Anne.

net netting, netted
Jimmy has **netted** a big fish.

nurse nursing, nursed
Mother **nursed** Andy when he had measles.

Oo

overturn
overturning, overturned
The boat **overturned** in the storm.

owe owing, owed
Peter borrows $1 from Jimmy.
He **owes** Jimmy $1.

open
opening, opened
Linda is **opening** her birthday presents.

operate operating, operated
The surgeon is **operating** on a man who has broken his leg.

63

overtake   overtaking, overtook
Our car is **overtaking** the truck.

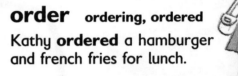

order   ordering, ordered
Kathy **ordered** a hamburger and french fries for lunch.

oil   oiling, oiled
Andy **oiled** the wheels of his toy car.

I'll help you repair your bicycle.

offer   offering, offered
Bobby **offered** to help Helen repair her bicycle.

own   owning, owned
Mandy saved up her money and now **owns** a new bicycle.

obey   obeying, obeyed
Mother said, 'Go to bed' and I had to **obey**.

occupy   occupying, occupied
Peter wanted to use the bathroom but it was **occupied**.

Pp

pierce piercing, pierced
The arrow **pierced** the apple.

paddle paddling, paddled
Bobby is **paddling** the canoe down the river.

pack packing, packed
Kathy is **packing** food for a picnic.

picnic picnicking, picnicked
The children are **picnicking** by the river.

pack up
The picnic is over.
The children are **packing up** the things.

peel peeling, peeled
Linda is **peeling** the orange.

peck pecking, pecked
The little bird is **pecking** at the apple.

poke poking, poked
Andy is **poking** a stick into the sand.

pluck plucking, plucked
Jimmy is busy **plucking** apples.

parachute parachuting, parachuted
Linda is **parachuting** into the forest.

pedal pedalling, pedalled
Bobby is **pedalling** his new bicycle up the hill.

peep peeping, peeped
Mandy is **peeping** through the window.

photograph
photographing, photographed
Jimmy is **photographing** the playful kitten.

pose posing, posed
Andy is **posing** for a photograph.

perch
perching, perched
The bird has **perched** on a branch.

pant panting, panted
The dog is **panting** after running up the steep slope.

pat patting, patted
Linda is **patting** the dog on the head.

paw pawing, pawed
The dog is **pawing** the rubber bone.

perform performing, performed
The magician is **performing** a trick.

park parking, parked
Mother **parked** the car next to a van.

patch patching, patched
Mother is **patching** a hole in the knee of Andy's jeans.

plant planting, planted
Mother is **planting** some daisy seeds in the garden.

pay paying, paid
Father is **paying** for the groceries at the check-out counter.

pay back
Jimmy is **paying back** the ten dollars Peter lent him.

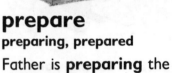

prepare
preparing, prepared
Father is **preparing** the fruit for dinner
He is cutting it.

peg pegged, pegging
Mother is **pegging** her washing.

present presenting, presented
Andy is **presenting** his mother with a bunch of roses.

place placing, placed
Mother **placed** the antique vase on the mantlepiece.

paint painting, painted
Andy is **painting** a picture of his family.

paste pasting, pasted
Bobby is **pasting** a poster on the wall.

pin pinning, pinned
Our teacher **pinned** a notice on the noticeboard.

pair pairing, paired
The socks are all mixed up. Can you **pair** them again?

part parting, parted
Terry always **parts** his hair on the left.

praise praising, praised
The teacher is **praising** Peter for the improvement in his school work.

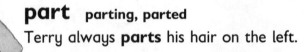

punish
punishing, punished
Andy was **punished** for being naughty.

play playing, played
Mandy and Kathy are **playing** hopscotch in the playground.

pretend pretending, pretended
Willy is **pretending** to be a ghost.

pound pounding, pounded
Mother is **pounding** the meat to make it tender.

powder
powdering, powdered
Aunt Molly is **powdering** her face.

pass passing, passed
Jimmy is **passing** the salt to Linda.

pinch pinching, pinched
A monster sneaked up and **pinched** my arm.

pile piling, piled
Jane is **piling** up the sand to make a sandcastle.

pick picking, picked
Jimmy is **picking** mangoes from a tree in his garden.

pick out
Mandy has **picked out** all the black jelly beans.

patrol patrolling, patrolled
Two policemen are **patrolling** our street.

pick up
Willy is **picking up** the pieces of broken glass.

69

polish polishing, polished
Father has washed the car.
He is now **polishing** it.

plough ploughing, ploughed
The farmer **ploughs** his field
before planting corn.

protect
protecting, protected
The shell of the snail
protects it from harm.

pave paving, paved
The workmen are **paving**
the road.

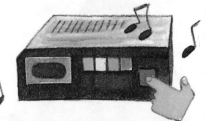

press pressing, pressed
Press this button to start
the machine.

prick pricking, pricked
A thorn **pricked** her finger
when Helen was cutting the
roses.

pull pulling, pulled
The elephant is **pulling** the
log out of the forest.

pull down
The workman is **pulling down** the house.

pull out
Andy's tooth was loose, so
the dentist **pulled** it **out**.

pour pouring, poured
Aunt Molly is **pouring** the tea into the cups.

pour on
Jimmy **poured** water **on** the fire to put it out.

purr purring, purred
Our cat **purrs** when you pat her.

pounce pouncing, pounced
The cat **pounced** on the mouse.

promise promising, promised
'I **promise** to look after it well,' said Simon.
'I will feed it and clean it.'

point pointing, pointed
Andy is **pointing** a finger at the puppies that chewed his father's slippers.

point out
The guide **pointed out** the old tower to the tourists.

pump pumping, pumped
Bobby **pumps** up his bicycle tyre.

post posting, posted
Kathy **posted** a letter to her French penpal.

71

practise   practising, practised
Kathy **practises** hard for a
ballet performance.

push   pushing, pushed
Jimmy is **pushing** the
box up the hill.

put   putting, put
Peter is **putting** his coins
into his money box.

put away
Helen **puts away**
her toys after playing
with them.

Qq

quack quack

quack

quack   quacking, quacked
The ducks **quack** when the farmer
comes to feed them.

Was the man
driving very
fast?

print   printing, printed
The machine **prints** posters.

puzzle   puzzling, puzzled
The men **puzzled** over the
huge footprint in the snow.

question
questioning, questioned
The policeman **questioned**
Jimmy to find out how the
accident happened.

Rr

quarter
quartering, quartered

Aunt Molly **quartered** the cake.

quarrel
quarrelling, quarrelled

Mandy and Helen are **quarrelling** over the torn storybook.

queue up

The children are **queuing up** to return their library books.

QUIET PLEASE

reach   reaching, reached

Linda can't **reach** the book on top of the bookcase.

renew   renewing, renewed

Willy had not finished his book, so he took it to the library and **renewed** it.

read   reading, read

Andy is **reading** *Treasure Island*.

raise   raising, raised

Peter has **raised** his hand. He knows the answer to the question.

relate   relating, related

Grandfather **related** the story of his childhood.

record
recording, recorded

Kathy **recorded** the day's events in her diary.

1st June Monday

73

rush — rushing, rushed
The ambulance is **rushing** a very sick man to hospital.

rain — raining, rained
It is **raining** very heavily so we cannot go outside.

report — reporting, reported
Uncle Roy **reported** to the police that his truck was stolen.

reverse — reversing, reversed
Mother is **reversing** the car. Get out of the way!

ram — ramming, rammed
Uncle Roy's truck **rammed** a bus.

repair — repairing, repaired
Our car would not start. The mechanic is **repairing** it.

replace — replacing, replaced
The mechanic **replaced** the spanner after he had used it. He put it back into the tool box.

run running, ran
Rusty can **run** very fast.

run out of
The car **ran out of** petrol in the middle of the road.

run over
The car **ran over** a watermelon and squashed it.

run into
The car **ran into** a lamp-post.

run away
The thief is **running away** with the jewels.

run after
Bobby **ran after** the thief, trying to catch him.

run in
The thief was **run in** for stealing the jewels.

request requesting, request
Hospital visitors are **requested** to leave by nine o'clock in the evening.

refuse refusing, refused
The camel **refuses** to stand up.

remind reminding, reminded
The tall, thin man **reminds** Mandy
of a giraffe.

race racing, raced
The hare and the tortoise are **racing** against
each other.

ride riding, rode
Jimmy **rides** a horse
very well.

release
releasing, released
Linda is **releasing**
the rabbit from
the cage.

roar roaring, roared
The lion is **roaring**
because he is angry.

repeat
repeating, repeated
The parrot is **repeating**
the same word over and
over again.

receive receiving, received
Andy **received** many presents
on his birthday.

remove removing, removed
Peter is **removing** his dirty
boots.

76

rake raking, raked

Grandfather is **raking** the leaves into a pile.

reflect reflecting, reflected

The moon is **reflected** in the lake.

regret

regretting, regretted

Andy **regrets** that he can't go on the picnic. He is sick.

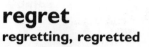

reserve reserving, reserved

This table is **reserved** for the Brown family.

rescue rescuing, rescued

The fireman **rescued** Jane from the fire.

ruffle ruffling, ruffled

Uncle Roy is **ruffling** Jimmy's hair.

reveal revealing, revealed

The artist removed the sheet and **revealed** the statue.

respect respecting, respected

Jimmy **respects** old people and gives them his seat on the bus.

ruin ruining, ruined

The painting was left out in the rain and was **ruined**.

77

What's your name?

Andy

reply replying, replied

'What's your name?' asked the robot.
'Andy,' I **replied**.

remain remaining, remained

Willy had four sweets.
He had eaten three.
One **remains**.

remember remembering, remembered

Father **remembered** it was mother's birthday.

row rowing, rowed

Jimmy is **rowing** the boat across the lake.

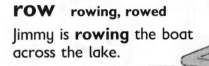

roller-skate roller-skating, roller-skated

Bobby is **roller-skating** down the path.

rest resting, rested

After hiking all day, Linda is **resting** her feet.

rub rubbing, rubbed

Willy **rubs** himself dry after his shower.

result resulting, resulted

The race **resulted** in a tie.
Bobby and Terry shared the first prize.

rip ripping, ripped

The naughty dog is **ripping** the curtain to pieces.

rub out

Mandy made a mistake but she **rubbed** it **out**.

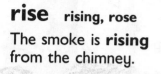

rise rising, rose

The smoke is **rising** from the chimney.

return returning, returned

Father **returns** from work at 5.30 p.m.

roast

roasting, roasted

Mother is **roasting** chestnuts over the fire.

ring ringing, rang

The bell **rings** when you press the button.

rock rocking, rocked

Kathy is **rocking** the baby in its cradle.

ring up

Kathy is **ringing up** her best friend to have a chat.

roll rolling, rolled

The ball is **rolling** down the hill.

roll up

Father is **rolling up** the carpet. He wants to vacuum under it.

rust rusting, rusted

Some of the nails have **rusted**.

ring off

Kathy is **ringing off** because her mother is calling her.

79

roam roaming, roamed

The girls are **roaming** around the park, looking at the flowers here and there.

rule ruling, ruled

The king **rules** his country wisely.

sag sagging, sagged

The top shelf **sags** because the books are too heavy.

rob robbing robbed

The thieves are **robbing** the man of his money.

scold scolding, scolded

The teacher is **scolding** Jimmy because he has not done his homework.

scream screaming, screamed

Mandy **screamed** when a bee landed on her arm.

scrub scrubbing, scrubbed

We **scrub** the floors to get them clean.

shape shaping, shaped

The potter is **shaping** the clay to make a pot.

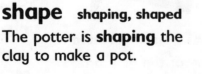

screw screwing, screwed

Uncle Roy is **screwing** the shelf to the wall.

save saving, saved

Terry **saves** ten cents from his pocket money every day.

save up

He wants to **save up** enough money to buy a pair of roller skates.

salute saluting, saluted

The children are **saluting** the flag.

score scoring, scored

Bobby **scored** a goal for his team.

scratch

scratching, scratched

The cat is **scratching** the flag pole to sharpen her claws.

scrape scraping, scraped

Jimmy fell down and **scraped** his knee.

scratch out

Kathy is **scratching out** the words so that no one can read them.

search searching, searched

Linda is **searching** everywhere to find the lost crayon.

select selecting, selected

The judge **selected** the best painting in the show.

sail sailing, sailed
Father is **sailing** his yacht around the buoy.

sink sinking, sank
The boat **sank** in the storm.

suck sucking, sucked
Terry is **sucking** the juice up through a straw.

scoop scooping, scooped
Jane **scooped** a bucketful of sand.

swim swimming, swam
Terry is **swimming** in the sea.

scoop out
Mother is **scooping out** ice-cream for the boys.

shout shouting, shouted
Willy is **shouting** for help. He cannot swim.

scoop up
Jimmy **scooped up** the kitten from the water.

splash splashing, splashed
Andy is **splashing** water on Helen's face.

say saying, said
Linda **says**, 'I'm going for a swim.'

I am going for a swim.

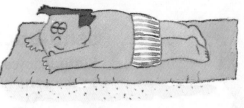

sun sunning, sunned

Willy is **sunning** himself on the beach.

strike striking, struck

Bobby **struck** the ball with his hand.

shade shading, shaded

The umbrella is **shading** Kathy from the sun.

smoke smoking, smoked

Grandfather is **smoking** a pipe.

skip skipping, skipped

Linda is **skipping** with her skipping rope.

spread spreading, spread

Father is **spreading** the cloth on the ground ready for the picnic.

share sharing, shared

Mandy and Helen are **sharing** the sweets.

sob sobbing, sobbed

Jane is **sobbing** because her sandcastle is ruined.

scare scaring, scared

Our fierce dog **scares** off Simon.

83

send sending, sent
Mother **sent** Andy to buy some sugar.

send back
Rusty followed Kathy to school so she **sent** him **back** home.

send off
The soccer player was **sent off** the field for kicking another player.

sell selling, sold
Simon helped his father **sell** oranges.

sell out
The oranges **sold out** in an hour.
There were none left.

set setting, set
Andy is **setting** the table for dinner.

set about
Andy **set about** his homework right after dinner.

set down
Willy **set down** his books on the desk.

set off
The boys **set off** on their hike at daybreak.

shear   shearing, sheared

The farmer is **shearing** a sheep.

shine   shining, shined

Jimmy **shines** his shoes every morning before school.

Dear Mandy,
  I'm terribly upset because the puppy you gave me has died suddenly.

        Peter

shock   shocking, shocked

The news **shocked** Mandy. She didn't expect such a terrible thing to happen.

seal   sealing, sealed

Peter put the letter in the envelope and **sealed** it.

sign   signing, signed

Peter **signed** his name at the bottom of the letter.

show   showing, showed

The salesman is **showing** Kathy some shoes.

shop   shopping, shopped

Linda is **shopping** for a pair of sunglasses.

show off

Kathy is **showing off** her new shoes.

show up

Jimmy **showed up** only after Helen had waited for him for an hour.

85

shake shaking, shook

Andy is **shaking** the medicine bottle to mix the medicine.

shake off

A spider landed on Mandy's hand but she **shook** it **off**.

separate separating, separated

Mother is **separating** the egg yolk from the egg white.

serve serving, served

Kathy is **serving** drinks to her guests.

sharpen sharpening, sharpened

Father is **sharpening** the carving knife carefully.

sit sitting, sat

Andy is **sitting** on the bean bag.

sit down

Jimmy **sat down** and watched television.

sew sewing, sewed

Grandmother **sewed** the button on my jacket.

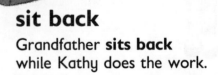

sit up

The teacher told Andy to **sit up** and pay attention.

sit back

Grandfather **sits back** while Kathy does the work.

shift shifting, shifted

Willy is **shifting** the armchair closer to the fireplace.

soak soaking, soaked

Bobby is **soaking** his sore feet in a bucket of hot water.

smooth
smoothing, smoothed

Kathy is **smoothing** out the wrinkles on the bed.

shower
showering, showered

You are dirty!
Go and **shower**.

sing singing, sang

Andy likes to **sing** in the shower.

shell shelling, shelled

Linda is **shelling** the nuts for the fruit cake.

shut shutting, shut

Kathy is **shutting** the window because the rain is coming in.

shut up

Andy has been talking for an hour.
His brother is getting tired and says, 'Please **shut up**!'

snore snoring, snored

Grandfather **snores** when he sleeps.

shovel
shovelling, shovelled

Father is **shovelling** snow away from the door.

ski skiing, skied
Jimmy learned to **ski** during his holiday in Switzerland.

skate skating, skated
The children are **skating** on a frozen pond.

shiver
shivering, shivered

It is so cold that Simon is **shivering**.

slap slapping, slapped
Jimmy **slapped** his friend on the back.

shrink shrinking, shrank
Willy's sweater **shrank** in the wash.
He cannot wear it anymore.

stamp
stamping, stamped

Helen is **stamping** her feet to keep warm.

step stepping, stepped
Mandy is **stepping** over the fallen log.

step in
Terry **stepped in** a puddle and got wet feet.

88

slope sloping, sloped
The path is **sloping** up the hill.

slide sliding, slid
Bobby is **sliding** down the
hill on a tyre.

spin spinning, spun
Can you **spin** on a frozen pond?

sniff sniffing, sniffed
The dog **sniffed** out the
rabbit.

surpise
surprising, surprised
Andy **surprised** Mandy
when he jumped out
from behind the
snowman.

snow snowing, snowed
It **snows** in winter and
you can make a snowman.

sneeze
sneezing, sneezed
Willy **sneezes** all the
time because he has
a cold.

achoOO

support supporting, supported
We **supported** Willy on each side
and helped him off the snow.

stare staring, stared
Linda is **staring** at the
chick in amazement.

89

shoot shooting, shot
Bobby **shoots** at the target twice.

shelter sheltering, sheltered
The sheep **sheltered** from the rain under the tree.

slip slipping, slipped
The clown **slipped** on the banana skin.

stink
stinking, stank
The rotting fish **stinks**.

spell spelling, spelt
Linda can **spell** her name.

slip off
Jimmy **slipped off** his shoes before entering the house.

slip under
Mandy is **slipping** a letter **under** the door.

snatch snatching, snatched
Andy **snatched** the toy from his sister.

slice slicing, sliced
Aunt Molly is **slicing** some bread for lunch.

smash smashing, smashed
Willy dropped a glass and it **smashed** onto the floor.

spray spraying, sprayed
Grandfather is **spraying** water on the plants.

sow sowing, sowed
Andy **sows** the seeds in the garden.

sweep sweeping, swept
Jimmy is **sweeping** the leaves from the path.

sprinkle sprinkling, sprinkled
Kathy is **sprinkling** water on the flowers.

see seeing, saw
Willy **sees** a caterpillar on the leaf.

spot spotting, spotted
Simon **spotted** a bug on another leaf.

swallow swallowing, swallowed
The snake **swallowed** a whole chicken.

sting stinging, stung
A bee **stung** Mandy on the finger.

smell smelling, smelled
Smell this and tell me what it is.

swell swelling, swelled
Mandy's finger **swelled** up after a bee stung her there.

91

spill spilling, spilt
The baby knocked its plate over and the food **spilt** onto the floor.

spring springing, sprang
The jack-in-the-box lid **sprang** open, making the baby laugh.

spoon spooning, spooned
Mother is **spooning** food into the baby's mouth.

I am....

speak speaking, spoke
Speak softly!
Baby is sleeping.

stuff stuffing, stuffed
Mother is **stuffing** the pillow with feathers.

sleep sleeping, slept
Babies look sweet when they are **sleeping**.

smile smiling, smiled
The baby **smiled** when it saw its father.

spit spitting, spat
The food tasted awful so Andy **spat** it out.

spank spanking, spanked
Father **spanked** Andy for tearing the book.

92

speed speeding, sped

Uncle Roy is **speeding** around the race track on his motorbike. See how fast he goes.

spend spending, spent

Jimmy has **spent** all his money. He has no money left.

split up

Terry and Andy talked in class so the teacher **split** them **up**.

split splitting, split

Father **split** the wood with an axe

stack stacking, stacked

Mandy is **stacking** her building blocks.

squat squatting, squatted

The policeman **squats** down to talk to the little lost girl.

steer steering, steered

You **steer** a horse with the reins.

squash squashing, squashed

Andy's car ran over a ball and **squashed** it.

spoil spoiling, spoilt

Willy's parents **spoil** him. They put the television and video recorder in his room.

store   storing, stored
The boxes are **stored** in the attic.

shave   shaving, shaved
Father **shaves** every morning.

squeeze
squeezing, squeezed
Willy is **squeezing** out some toothpaste.

shampoo
shampooing, shampooed
Kathy is **shampooing** her hair.

stay   staying, stayed
Grandfather has come to **stay** with us for the weekend.

stay up
Andy **stayed up** till midnight to finish reading the ghost story.

stay in
Helen had to **stay in** after school to do her homework.

stay out
The boys **stayed out** in the garden all night.

stay away
'**Stay away** from the fire,' said Aunt Molly. 'You might get burnt.'

steal
stealing, stole
The burglar is **stealing** the silver.

sound sounding, sounded
The alarm clock **sounded** at six o'clock.

start starting, started
Grandmother **started** knitting a jumper but she hasn't finished it yet.

stretch stretching, stretched
Willy gets out of bed and **stretches** himself.

stick sticking, stuck
Kathy is **sticking** a stamp on the envelope.

stoop
stooping, stooped
Andy **stoops** down to pick up the pencil.

stir stirring, stirred
Kathy is **stirring** the soup on the stove.

stick up
'Stick up your hands!' said the robber.

stick out
Andy is **sticking out** his tongue at his friend.

stick together
The pieces of the broken vase have been **stuck together** with glue.

stand for
What colour **stands for** danger?

stand
standing, stood
Andy **stands** on the stool to reach the cookie jar.

stand back
The policeman told everyone to **stand back** from the monster.

stand up
Stand up and give your seat to the old gentleman.

stitch
stitching, stitched
Grandmother **stitched** a pretty bow on the collar of the dress.

stitch up
My hem came undone, so I **stitched** it **up**.

stop
stopping, stopped
Our car **stopped** at the red light.

stop up
Bobby **stopped up** the hole in the wall with cardboard.

string
stringing, stringed
Linda is **stringing** the beads to make a necklace.

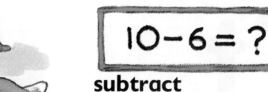

surround surrounding, surrounded

Sharks **surrounded** the boat.

subtract

subtracting, subtracted

Can you **subtract** six from ten?

study studying, studied

Every night Peter **studies** for his exam.

succeed

succeeding, succeeded

Peter **succeeded** in passing his exam.

suit suiting, suited

This dress doesn't **suit** Aunt Molly.
It makes her look fat.

sweat

sweating, sweated

The runners are **sweating**.

swing swinging, swung

The monkey is **swinging** from one bar to another.

switch switching, switched

The clowns **switched** their hats, making the people laugh.

switch off

Mother **switched off** the light before leaving the room.

switch on

Jimmy **switched on** the television.

T t

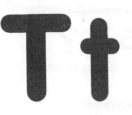

teach   teaching, taught

Grandmother is **teaching** Kathy how to knit.

thread   threading, threaded

Aunt Molly **threaded** the needle to do some sewing.

$$5 + 2 = 7 \checkmark$$
$$10 - 7 = 3 \checkmark$$
$$6 + 2 = 9 \times$$
$$11 + 4 = 15 \checkmark$$

tick   ticking, ticked

The teacher **ticked** all the sums that were correct.

tap   tapping, tapped

Linda **tapped** Andy on his shoulder to get his attention.

telephone
telephoning, telephoned

The house is on fire! **Telephone** the fire brigade.

List
sugar ✓
bread ✓
canned food
blanket ✓
rope
coffee ✓
cookies ✓
torch
knife ✓
matches ✓

tick off

Benny **ticked off** the things on the list that he has got for the camp.

test   testing, tested

The doctor is **testing** Bobby's eyes to see if he needs glasses.

tidy   tidying, tidied

The desk was a mess so Kathy **tidied** it up.

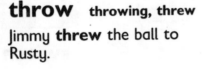

throw   throwing, threw

Jimmy **threw** the ball to Rusty.

throw away

The radio was broken so Andy **threw** it **away**.

tie   tying, tied
Scouts learn to **tie** different knots.

tie up
We are playing cops and robbers.
We are **tying up** the robber so he can't escape.

tighten
tightening, tightened
Willy **tightens** the knot to make sure that the rope will not slip off the tree.

tour   touring, toured
Mandy is **touring** France with a friend.

touch   touching, touched
Bend down and **touch** your toes.

touch down
Our aeroplane **touched down** at the airport on time.

time   timing, timed
Jimmy is running round the field.
Father is **timing** him.

tip   tipping, tipped
Father **tipped** the waiter for being every helpful.

tip over
The bottle **tipped over** and the ketchup spilt on the carpet.

toast   toasting, toasted
Linda is **toasting** bread for breakfast.

99

thank thanking, thanked
Jane **thanked** Peter for the birthday present.

tear tearing, tore
Jimmy **tore** his coat on a nail.

tear up
Linda didn't like her drawing, so she **tore** it **up**.

tear out
Bobby **tore out** a photograph from the newspaper.

trick tricking, tricked
Andy **tricked** Linda with a plastic spider.

Happy Birthday - Jane

talk talking, talked
The parrot can **talk**.

take off
Kathy is **taking off** her coat.

take taking, took
Willy is **taking** the cookies from the jar.

take up
Mandy wants to **take up** ballet.

think
thinking, thought

Terry **thought** of what he wanted for his birthday.

think up

Mandy **thought up** a good costume for the fancy dress party.

try on

Kathy is **trying on** a beautiful party dress.

toss
tossing, tossed

Helen and Willy are **tossing** the ball to each other.

try
trying, tried

Benny is **trying** to lift the weights but he can't.

tickle
tickling, tickled

Bobby **tickled** Andy's feet to make him laugh.

taste
tasting, tasted

Lemons **taste** sour.

twist
twisting, twisted

Willy **twisted** the cap to open the bottle.

tell
telling, told

Simon is **telling** Kathy about his trip to Switzerland.

turn turning, turned

Mandy is blowing the windmill.
See how it **turns**!

turn back

The path is blocked so Jimmy has to **turn back**.

turn down

Father asked Andy to **turn down** the radio because it was too loud.

turn on

Mother **turned on** the television to watch the news.

turn off

Turn off the bath water before it overflows.

turn up

Jimmy **turned up** late for the party.

turn round

The ballet dancer is **turning round** and round.

tremble
trembling, trembled

Andy **trembled** when he saw a monster coming towards him.

twinkle
twinkling, twinkled

The stars **twinkle** in the clear sky.

102

trap trapping, trapped
The fox is **trapped** by its tail.

train training, trained
The trainer is **training** the elephant to stand on its back legs.

trip tripping, tripped
Andy **tripped** over a stone.

tiptoe tiptoeing, tiptoed
The burglar is **tiptoeing** down the hall.

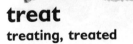

treat
treating, treated
Linda **treats** her pet rabbit very well. She feeds it and cleans its cage every day.

trim trimming, trimmed
Grandfather is **trimming** the hedge.

travel travelling, travelled
Kathy **travels** to school by bus.

trace tracing, traced
Andy is **tracing** a picture of a dinosaur.

type typing, typed
The secretary is **typing** a letter.

tuck tucking, tucked
Mother is **tucking** the blanket in around the baby.

Uu

understand
understanding, understood

Bobby doesn't **understand** why the television won't work.

underline
underlining, underlined

Kathy is **underlining** all the important words.

I pushed my bicycle up

unload **unloading, unloaded**

The strong men are **unloading** the piano off the truck.

upset **upsetting, upset**

The cat **upset** the bowl of fish.

urge **urging, urged**

Jimmy **urged** the dog to jump across the water.

unfasten
unfastening, unfastened

When the car stops you **unfasten** the safety belt.

unlock
unlocking, unlocked

Father is **unlocking** the door.

untie **untying, untied**

Untie your shoelaces before you take your shoes off.

undress undressing, undressed

Kathy got **undressed** ready for her bath.

unpack unpacking, unpacked

Mandy **unpacks** her suitcase after her trip.

unwrap unwrapping, unwrapped

Linda is **unwrapping** her Christmas present.

use using, used

Andy is **using** a blue crayon to colour the car.

unroll unrolling, unrolled

Andy is **unrolling** his painting.

Vv

vacuum vacuuming, vacuumed

Aunt Molly is **vacuuming** the room.

use up

The milk is **used up**. We must buy some more.

visit visiting, visited

We **visited** Grandma at the hospital this afternoon.

vanish vanishing, vanished

The magician waved his wand and the rabbit **vanished**.

Ww

wade   wading, waded
Jimmy is **wading** across the water.

wag   wagging, wagged
The puppy is **wagging** its tail happily.

waddle
waddling, waddled
A duck **waddles**.

walk   walking, walked
Grandfather is **walking** in the park.

wake   waking, woke
Be quiet!
Don't **wake** the baby.

POW
WOW
POW

walk off with
Andy **walked off with** the first prize in the painting contest.

wake up
The baby **woke up** because Andy was making a lot of noise.

wait   waiting, waited
Bobby is **waiting** at the bus stop for the bus to arrive.

warm   warming, warmed
We are **warming** ourselves round the fire.

wander   wandering, wandered
Simon and Linda are **wandering** through the woods. They are lost.

106

wash washing, washed

Linda **washed** her hands after playing with the clay.

warn
warning, warned

The red light **warns** you when the machine gets too hot.

wash up

Kathy **washes up** the dishes after dinner.

waste wasting, wasted

Turn off the lights so you don't **waste** electricity.

water watering, watered

Mandy **waters** her plants every day.

weep weeping, wept

Jane is **weeping** over her broken doll.

watch over

The mother hen **watches over** her chickens to make sure they are safe.

watch watching, watched

Bobby is **watching** a game of football on television.

watch out

You must **watch out** for cars when you cross the road.

wave waving, waved

Kathy is **waving** goodbye to her friend.

107

wear wearing, worn
Kathy is **wearing** her mother's shoes.

wear out
Jimmy's shoes have holes in them. They are **worn out**.

wheel
wheeling, wheeled
The nurse is **wheeling** Willy down the corridor.

whip whipping, whipped
Linda is **whipping** the cream for the apple pie.

weigh weighing, weighed
The butcher is **weighing** the meat.

whistle
whistling, whistled
Jimmy is **whistling** for his dog.

wet wetting, wetted
Bobby **wet** his shoes when he stepped into a puddle.

whisper whispering, whispered
Whisper the secret so only I can hear you.

win winning, won
My pet dog **won** first prize at the dog show.

weave weaving, wove
Mandy is **weaving** a basket.

welcome
welcoming, welcomed
Kathy **welcomes** her aunt with flowers.

108

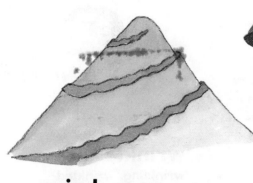

wind winding, wound
The road **winds** around the hill.

wind up
Father **winds up** the grandfather clock once a week.

wink winking, winked
Willy **winked** at me.

wish wishing, wished
Andy **wished** that he had never gone for a ride with Uncle Roy.

work
working, worked
Mr Hart **works** as an engine driver.

$$1003 \times 4$$

work out
The teacher is **working out** the answer to the sum on the blackboard.

wriggle wriggling, wriggled
The worms **wriggled** around in the jar.

wipe wiping, wiped
Andy is **wiping** his wet hands on the cloth.

wring wringing, wrung
Mother is **wringing** the water out of the cloth.

wound
wounding, wounded
The soldier was **wounded** in the shoulder.

109

worry worrying, worried
Andy is **worried** about his sick grandmother.

wrap wrapping, wrapped
Mandy is **wrapping** up the birthday present.

wrinkle
wrinkling, wrinkled
When Uncle Tom frowns he **wrinkles** his forehead.

wonder
wondering, wondered
Simon can't find his cat. He **wonders** where she is.

write writing, wrote
Linda is **writing** a letter to her cousin.

write down
Aunt Molly is **writing down** the shopping list so she will not forget what to buy.

Yy

yawn yawning, yawned
When you are tired you **yawn**.

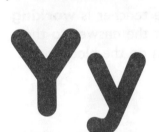

yell yelling, yelled
That baby is **yelling** for his mother.

Zz

zip zipping, zipped
Jimmy **zipped** up his jacket.

zoom zooming, zoomed
The car **zoomed** past us.